LEICESTERSHIRE
Ghost Stories

Prepare to be frightened by these terrifying
tales from around Leicestershire

By

David Bell

BRADWELL
BOOKS

Published by Bradwell Books
9 Orgreave Close Sheffield S13 9NP

Email: books@bradwellbooks.co.uk
© David Bell 2013

British Library Cataloguing in Publication Data: a catalogue
record for this book is available from the British Library.
1st Edition

ISBN: 9781902674636

Print: Gomer Press, Llandysul, Ceredigion SA44 4JL

Design by: jenksdesign@yahoo.co.uk

CONTENTS

Introduction 5

Grace Dieu Priory: *Thringstone* 6

The Grey Hangman's Stone: *Shepshed* 8

Five-to-Four Fred: *Newton Burgoland* 11

The Witches of Belvoir Castle 14

Swithland The Lady in Grey 20

The Legend of Red Comyn 23

The Black Boy of Wanlip 26

The White Horse of Leesthorpe Hill 29

The Haunted Police Station: *Syston* 31

Black Annis: *Dane Hills* 34

The Cat And The Cleaver: *Edmonthorpe* 39

The Bleeding Tomb: *Hinckley* 42

The Haunted Theatre: *Market Harborough* 45

Butterfly Hall: *Lubbenham* 49

Braunstone Hall 54

The Haunted Railway Line: Wykin 57

Caught on Camera: *Belgrave Hall* 60

The Battle of Bosworth Revisited 63

Esmeralda, The Gypsy Girl: Stoke Golding 66

Topsy Turvey: *Bilstone* 68

Footsteps and a screaming baby: Breedon-On-The-Hill 73

Ghost on a bike: *Measham* 75

The Ghost of a Nine-Days-Queen 77

Bibiography 79

INTRODUCTION

Leicestershire has many places connected with tales of ghosts. Many are in places where you might expect haunting. Anyone driving along the A512 from Loughborough to Ashby-de-la-Zouch, and catching sight of the ruins of Grace Dieu priory, will know immediately that there has to be a ghost story connected with it. They will be right.

Many of the county's ancient houses, including Braunstone Hall and Belgrave Hall, have a number of ghosts in residence. Even some of the demolished houses – Papillon Hall and Edmonthorpe Hall – have left their ghosts around where the houses once stood. The recent discovery of the body of Richard III, who died in battle in Leicestershire, has led to reports of many haunting connected with him.

But there are also several haunted pubs, a haunted theatre and a haunted police station. In Bottesford village church in the north of the county, there is a memorial bearing a unique reference to children being killed by "wicked practice and sorcerye," the only mention of witchcraft in any English church.

In the west of the county, passers-by travelling from Twycross to Bilstone can still see a gibbet post, unsurprisingly situated on Gibbet Lane. On the information board attached to it, they can discover that the last man to have his body displayed on the post was suspended there for eighteen years.

Add to the mix the ghost of a cycling miner seen in Measham, a tomb that bleeds every April in Hinckley, and a male chauvinist ghost that smothers men but strokes women, and you will see that Leicestershire has a rich and varied heritage of places for the ghost hunter to visit.

David Bell

GRACE DIEU PRIORY: *Thringstone*

The ruins of Grace Dieu Priory, a former nunnery, stand in the grounds of a Roman Catholic prep school, near Thringstone. The resident ghost there is a lady dressed in white. Charlie Gough, a gardener on the estate before the time of the school, saw the ghost of a white lady on many occasions. She was wearing a white robe and a hat with a wide brim.

In 1954, the driver of a bus travelling from Thringstone to Shepshed stopped to pick up a nun dressed in white at the bus stop opposite the ruins. When the conductor opened the door for her to get on, she disappeared. The driver and conductor searched but there was no sign of her.

It was an off-duty policeman walking his dog in the field about half a mile from the ruins who met her in the spring of 1961. His dog growled and the hair on its neck stood up when they saw what the man described as 'a white form in the shape of a cloak and hood'. He said that the apparition glided right past him and vanished through a hedge.

Vince Ball, a nurse at Loughborough Hospital, saw her in 1986. He was riding his motorbike past the ruins of Grace Dieu Priory when he saw a luminous figure crossing the road. He stopped, as did the driver of the car in front of him. Each of them asked the other to confirm what they had witnessed. Both of them had seen the White Lady.

It has recently been discovered that the nuns at Grace Dieu wore white habits, unlike the more common black habits worn by most Augustinian nuns. This has led people to believe that the ghost is that of a former nun. Some claim that she is the ghost of a novice nun who was unhappy with her vocation. One winter night she decided to run away, to get back to her family home at Belton, but she got lost in a snowstorm and died of exposure to the cold.

Others insist that she is in fact Agnes Litherland, the prioress at the time the priory was closed down by Henry VIII. There is a

Ruins of Grace Dieu Priory
(photo by David Bell)

story that Agnes had hidden the priory treasure in a secret tunnel under the building, to prevent it from falling into the hands of the soldiers. When she refused to say where the treasure was, she was slain by the soldiers.

Either way, whether an unhappy novice or a brave prioress, her ghost can still be seen in the ruins of Grace Dieu Priory.

THE GREY HANGMAN'S STONE: *Shepshed*

Ives Head and Lubcloud are hills that slope down to the southern edge of Shepshed, and on Lubcloud there is a rock that projects from the ground. It is known as the Grey Hangman's Stone, and the story behind it is a macabre one.

The villages of Shepshed and Whitwick were always renowned for producing families of poachers. I have taught in a school in Whitwick and there could well be another generation coming up.

An ancient poem stated

> What matter that wardens and trusty regarders
> Looked well to the forest right;
> The Shepshed encroachers were all practised
> poachers
> And their day was the noon of the night.

The Grey Hangman's Stone on Lubcloud
(photo © Bob Trubshaw)

There was plenty of game to poach in the area between the two villages: trout in Carly Brook, hares and rabbits on Warren Hills, herons on High Sharpley and goats and hogs at Ives Head. If these proved elusive, there were always herds of deer in Charnwood Forest.

One expert poacher was John of Oxley. He'd left his home in Shepshed, checked his traps, which were empty, and wandered into the forest. He tracked a herd of deer, then drew an arrow from his quiver. One arrow from his yew longbow brought down a fine hart. To carry it home, he tied its back legs together, slipped them over his head and hoisted the deer onto his back.

Cheerfully he strode down Lubcloud, no doubt thinking how pleased his wife would be with the venison they'd be dining on in the weeks to come. He was looking forward to the mulled ale that she always had waiting for him. The weight of the deer on his back was heavy and he paused by an upright stone and rested his burden on it.

As his wife waited for John's return in their Shepshed home, she became worried as the night wore on. He was not back at daylight. She waited all the next day, and for another night. She knew in her heart that something dreadful must have happened to her husband.

> Days passed and he came not; his children played
> And wept, then played again.
> They saw with wet eyes that their mother's sad eyes
> Were still on the hills, in vain.

It was two days before the mystery was solved. A swineherd walking down Lubcloud saw a man standing on his own. He called out but the man didn't reply. Striding over to him, he was horrified to see that although the man was standing upright, he was stone dead.

It was John of Oxley, the Shepshed poacher. He had rested the deer on the standing stone, but the dead animal had slipped down behind the rock, and its tied feet had tightened around John's neck. The animal he'd killed had taken its revenge and throttled him.

> All was clear, there was Oxley one side the stone
> On the other the down-hanging deer.
> The burden had slipped and his neck it had nipped!
> He was hanged by his prize, it was clear.

The rock is still there on Lubcloud Hill and is known as the Grey Hangman's Stone. Lubcloud is said to be haunted by the ghost of John of Oxley, the poacher strangled by his prey.

FIVE-TO-FOUR FRED: *Newton Burgoland*

In Newton Burgoland there is a pub called the Belper Arms, Leicestershire's oldest tavern. The stonemasons who built Swepstone church in the twelfth century lodged there, although it was then known as The Shepherd and Shepherdess.

The Belper Arms has a resident ghost who has been nicknamed Five-to-Four Fred, as he only manifests himself at 3.55am or 3.55pm. No one has ever seen or heard the ghost, so how does he make himself known?

The Belper Arms at Newton Burgoland
(photo by David Bell)

It has to be said that Fred isn't a new man; he is an old-fashioned male chauvinist ghost. He treats men and women very differently. If a man experiences the presence of Fred, he has the sensation of having hands placed over his nose and mouth, trying to smother him. I have spoken to two men who've had this experience. One was a former landlord of the Belper Arms, who woke in the night – presumably it was five to four – when he felt hands over his nose and mouth. I did of course ask him if it might have been his wife, but he denied this. 'No, she was snoring away next to me,' he said. 'It was definitely Fred trying to do me in.'

The other man was a patron of the pub. He told me that, at closing time, the landlord took his car keys off him and said that he could sleep in the warm bar. His version was that it had been snowing and the landlord didn't want him driving home in the snow. Actually, I wonder whether in fact the landlord thought he'd drunk too much beer. Whatever the reason, the man slept in the deserted bar until he was awoken in the early hours by someone trying to smother him. 'I were that frit, me duck,' he told me, 'I let meself out of the pub and shivered in me cold car until it was light enough to drive home.'

That's what happens if you're male. For women, it is a different tale. If Five-to-Four Fred decides to make himself known to a lady, she has the sensation of having her face stroked or her bottom patted!

Fred is said to be the ghost of a highwayman who was courting a serving wench – a barmaid – from the pub. One day when he came home from work – robbing, etc. – he found that his sweetheart had been murdered, and her body thrown down a well.

The highwayman's ghost is said to be still looking for the man who did the murder, and that is why he tries to smother men. He is also still looking for his old sweetheart, hence the familiarity he shows to women.

I'm not sure whether the chaps who drink in the Belper Arms get falsely accused by ladies who think they're being stroked or patted by a living hand. Or is it possible that the men who drink there use this legend to misbehave?

THE WITCHES OF
BELVOIR CASTLE

In St Mary's Church in Bottesford, on the monument of Francis, the sixth Earl of Rutland, the following words are recorded:

IN 1605 HE MARRIED LADY CECELIA
HUNGERFORD
DAUGHTER TO YE HONBLE KNIGHT SIR
JOHN TUFTON
BY WHOM HE HAD TWO SONS
BOTH WHICH DIED IN THEIR INFANCY
BY WICKED PRACTICE AND SORCERYE

This makes Bottesford church unique, because it is the only English church to contain within its walls any reference to sorcery.

The witches referred to are Joan Flower and her two daughters, Margaret and Philippa. Joan Flower was reputed to be a witch because she had an ugly face, a harsh voice, she swore and she never went to church. I'm thinking that description would include quite a few of us today.

Her daughter Philippa had been accused of witchcraft on completely different grounds by a local man, Thomas Simpson. His account – a man's excuse if ever I heard one – was that Philippa had bewitched him into falling in love with her to such a degree that he couldn't control his mind or his body! I think it is safe to assume that Philippa was prettier than her mother.

The monument in Bottesford Church which refers to deaths
by witchcraft and sorcery
(photo by David Bell)

Joan's other daughter, Margaret, went into service at Belvoir Castle as a laundress and poultrymaid, but the girl was dismissed after a few months for stealing food.

The Earl then suffered a double tragedy. His oldest son, Henry, Lord Rosse, became ill and died. Next his younger son Francis fell ill. He also died. The Earl's daughter Katherine was taken ill too, but she recovered from her illness, but that was no compensation for his loss. He had lost 'his heir and his spare', as the two eldest sons of any nobleman were called.

Thrashing around in his grief for someone to blame, he remembered the sacking of the laundrymaid who came from a family of witches. The first decades of the seventeenth century were very much obsessed with seeking for witches. One of the monarchs who was particularly harsh on witches was James I. The Elizabethan age had been fairly moderate in its attitudes to witchcraft, the queen refusing to condemn alleged witches to death. However, when James VI of Scotland succeeded to the English throne he turned the clock back in that respect. He even wrote a book called Daemonologie, urging his subjects to seek out witches and bring them to trial. Before coming to the English throne he'd had 1500 Scottish women put to death as witches. The king was obsessed with witches, so it soon spread to other members of the aristocracy – including Earl Francis – then to the common people.

Joan Flower and her two daughters were arrested, together with Anne Baker of Bottesford, Joan Willimot of Goadby and Ellen Greene of Stathern. They were all taken in for questioning. The allegation against the three members of the Flower family was that they had stolen a glove belonging to the Earl's eldest boy, boiled it, pricked it many times with a knife, rubbed it on the back of their cat, called Rutterkin, then buried it in a manure heap. As the glove rotted away, the boy was taken ill and died. They repeated it with a glove of the younger son and he too died.

Belvoir Castle
(Photo reproduced with kind permission of their graces
the Duke and Duchess of Rutland).

THE
WONDERFVL
DISCOVERIE OF THE
Witchcrafts of *Margaret* and *Phillip*
Flower, daughters of *Joan Flower* neere *Beuer*
Castle: executed at Lincolne, *March* ii. 1618.

Who were specially arraigned & condemned before
Sir *Henry Hobart*, and Sir *Edward Bromley*, Judges
of Assize, for confessing themselues actors in the destruc-
tion of *Henry*, Lord *Rosse*, with their damnable prac-
tises against others the Children of the Right
Honourable FRANCIS Earle of *Rutland*.

Together with the seuerall Examinations and Confessions of *Anne
Baker*, *Ioan Willimot*, and *Ellen Greene*, Witches in *Leicestershire*.

Printed at London by *G. Eld* for *I. Barnes*, dwelling in the long Walke
neere Christ-Church. 1619.

*The front cover of a pamphlet detailing the trial of the Belvoir witches.
It was published in 1619 and shows Anne Baker, Joan Willimot and
Ellen Greene.*

The pamphlet of 1619

They tried the same thing with a handkerchief belonging to Katherine, the Earl's young daughter. They boiled it and pricked it, but when they went to rub it on Rutterkin, the cat ran away. They buried it anyway, but they'd missed out that vital step. Katherine recovered.

The other allegation against the Flowers was that they took some wool from the bed of the Earl and Countess. They boiled it in blood, dried it out, and then surreptitiously put it back in the bed. Somehow, this prevented the Earl and his wife from conceiving any more children! The allegation was now that they had caused the death of his two sons, and prevented him from having any more. This was obviously treason as well as witchcraft.

When I say that the women were taken in for questioning, that is a euphemism. What happened to the six women in the days and weeks that followed can only be imagined. They were obviously cruelly treated, and almost certainly tortured. Certainly by the time they were brought before the Judges of the Assizes in February and March, they were ready to make confessions.

Joan Flower, the mother, died in prison. The story put out by the authorities was that she was eating some bread, when she said, 'If I am guilty of witchcraft, may I be struck down on the spot.' Immediately she choked to death on the bread.

This, in the early 1600s, was held to be direct proof of her guilt and, by association, that of her daughters too. They were taken out and publicly hanged as witches. We did not in England burn witches at the stake. We reserved that for heretics – being Catholic under Henry VIII or Protestant under Queen Mary.

The fate of Anne Baker, Joan Willimot and Ellen Greene – accused of lesser crimes – is not known, although it is possible that they too were hanged as witches.

A pamphlet was published in 1619, giving details of the witchcraft of Joan, Philippa and Margaret Flower, describing their confession to their alleged 'wicked practice and sorcery'. But were they truly guilty?

Perhaps not, because the ghosts of the three women, Joan Flower and her daughters, still haunt the grounds of Belvoir Castle. Moreover, they are still protesting their innocence of the crimes they were accused of by their cruel master, Francis, the sixth Earl of Rutland.

THE LADY IN GREY: *Swithland*

The legend of the Lady in Grey harks back to a tragic event that took place in Swithland almost two hundred years ago. The family who lived in the old rectory had been on holiday in Yorkshire. The daughter, a pretty girl of twenty, was unhappy when her father ordered her to return to the rectory a day ahead of the rest of the family, in order to ensure that everything at the rectory was ready for them. Despite her misgivings, the girl

Swithland old Rectory
(from the photograph collection of Joan Leatherland).

felt that she must obey her father's wishes. She travelled by stagecoach to Loughborough, alighting at the Plough Inn in the Market Place in the mid-afternoon. She then hired a private carriage to complete the journey to Swithland.

Once home, she was very alarmed by the appearance of the family butler. His eyes were heavy and bloodshot, and he was staggering around as if he were drunk, or possibly insane. Although he spoke respectfully to her, she remained apprehensive and decided to stay awake all night. She did not undress, but lay down on her bed, still wearing the grey brocade dress in which she had travelled home.

Despite her vow to stay awake, her eyes closed and she fell asleep. In the early hours, she was suddenly awakened by the sound of her bedroom door being forced open. She saw the butler approaching her. He seemed to be now completely out of his senses. He seized her, and easily overpowered her.

Some time later, the man's senses returned, and a scene of utter horror met his eyes. He saw the girl's dead body hanging from a rope from the top of the four-poster bed. He realised that he had murdered her. He rushed to the kitchen, seized a large meat knife and cut his own throat. The two bodies were discovered the next day when the family returned.

For the next hundred years, local people reported hearing terrible screams coming from the rectory at night. A few

Swithland Church
(from the photograph collection of Joan Leatherland).

villagers claimed to have seen the ghost of the butler with blood streaming from his throat, groaning with remorse and guilt.

These hauntings ceased when the rectory was demolished after World War I, but the Lady in Grey is still seen in the locality. Sometimes she walks in the churchyard at night, but she has also been observed in daylight, appearing at garden parties and other social events. She is always wearing her dress of grey brocade.

THE LEGEND OF RED COMYN: *Whitwick*

In 1551, Lady Jane Grey – the great-niece of Henry VIII – was walking in the grounds of Bradgate Hall with Francis Beaumont of Grace Dieu Hall. They were both 14, and it's possible that they were childhood sweethearts, though Jane's father had plans to marry her much more highly and then to make her Queen of England.

Suddenly they were attacked by a huge red wolf. It knocked Francis to the ground, then turned to Jane. She picked up a branch and thrust it into the snarling open mouth, and the wolf was killed. Lady Jane Grey had slain the last wild wolf in Leicestershire.

This legend may have a connection with another Leicestershire story. In 1304 the Lord of Whitwick Castle was one Red Comyn, a giant of a man with long red hair and beard. His three great interests were drinking, fighting and womanising. No local maiden was safe from his clutches.

One girl who took his fancy was Agnes, the young daughter of Lord Ferrars of Groby Hall, but she refused his advances. One Sunday morning in 1304, Lord Comyn sent his men to seize her and bring her back to Whitwick, but she managed to evade them. When Red Comyn heard, he flew into a rage and promised a reward to the man who brought her to him but a hanging for all those who failed.

In a thunderstorm, Agnes fled through Charnwood Forest with Comyn's men in pursuit. On Buck Hill, near Nanpantan, she realised they were very near, and she hid in a hollow oak tree. Agnes could hear her brutal pursuers searching for her. She prayed that she should remain safe from the lustful intentions of Red Comyn. Eventually the men left and she continued her escape.

Early next morning, a hermit, who lived in an enclosure called Holy Well Haw, saw the body of a girl lying on the ground. He carried her to the well and sprinkled water over her deathly white face. To his joy, he saw her eyelids flutter and her lips move. He sent word back to Lord Ferrars, and the girl was taken back to Groby Hall.

The next spring, the same hermit saw a young couple riding on horseback towards him. After each drinking a shellful of water from the well, they introduced themselves. The young man said that his name was Edward Grey, and that the girl was his bride, Agnes, the same girl the hermit had helped the previous year.

The Farmhouse at Holy Well Haw

A hermitage since the early 1100s, Holy Well Haw is now a farmhouse, but the water from the well – actually a spring – still flows. Visiting it in April 2002, I was given a drink of water from the well and it was as cold and pure as it was in the days of Agnes Ferrars and Red Comyn.

The wild behaviour of Red Comyn continued throughout his life. He died in a fight at the age of 34, but after his death a new and terrifying story began to spread. In the forest, a huge wolf was lurking. This wolf had a taste for the flesh of young maidens, and moreover the creature was covered in long red fur. The belief grew that the wolf was in fact Red Comyn, and that the only way the wolf could die was by the hand of a virtuous young maiden of royal blood. Jane was that royal maiden, and moreover she was a descendant of Agnes Ferrars, who had evaded the lustful intentions of Red Comyn 150 years earlier.

THE BLACK BOY OF WANLIP

Cliff Lewis was driving from Syston to his home in Birstall one foggy night in November 1989. He was driving very slowly because of the weather, when the figure of a young black boy appeared in front of him in the village of Wanlip. He braked, but it was too late. Thinking that he'd hit the lad, Cliff stopped the car and got out.

There was no sign of the boy, either lying on the road or sitting injured at the roadside. He called out into the fog, 'Are you all right?' but there was no answer. He put on his hazard flashers and walked twenty or thirty yards up the road. He thought he saw an orange light in a field over a low stone wall. He called out again, but as there was no answer, he walked back to his car and drove on. After a stiff drink, he went to bed, still convinced that he'd hit and hurt the boy.

The next day he went back to the spot where the accident had occurred. He asked around the village but nobody had heard of anyone being hurt the day before. When he described the boy – a young black boy of about twelve or thirteen – he got a few funny looks. Eventually, one villager told him to go and look in the village churchyard. There, on the left of the footpath, he found the gravestone he'd been told to look for.

On the tombstone, under a symbol of a circle with wings, he read the inscription:

> SACRED TO THE MEMORY OF RASSELAS
> MORJAN
> WHO WAS BORN IN MACADI
> IN THE CONFINES OF ABYSSINIA
> AND DIED AT WANLIP HALL
> AUGUST 25TH 1839
> IN THE 19TH YEAR OF HIS LIFE
>
> RESCUED FROM A STATE OF SLAVERY
> IN THIS LIFE
> AND ENABLED BY GOD'S GRACE
> TO BECOME A MEMBER OF HIS CHURCH
> HE RESTS HERE IN THE HOPE
> OF A GREATER DELIVERANCE HEREAFTER
>
> THIS STONE IS RAISED
> IN REMEMBRANCE OF HIS BLAMELESS LIFE
> BY ONE WHOM HE LOVED

The tombstone of Rassalas Morjan
(photo by David Bell)

Geoff Allan, a former resident of Wanlip, told me that Wanlip Hall was demolished in 1935. He added that the bungalow that stands on the site of the hall has had a series of families living there, as no one ever stays for more than a year, because the place is haunted.

Cliff Lewis is convinced that the boy he ran into on that foggy November night was, in fact, the ghost of Rasselas Morjan, the freed slave, wandering through a Leicestershire village thousands of miles from his native Africa.

He admires the owners of Wanlip Hall for rescuing the boy from slavery and taking him to live in the Hall, but added, 'Wouldn't it have been better to say that the gravestone was raised by one who loved him, rather than by one whom he loved?'

THE WHITE HORSE OF LEESTHORPE HILL

The ghostly white horse that glides over the road at Leesthorpe Hill, seven miles south-east of Melton Mowbray, has a tragic story attached to it. The magnificent horse belonged to a warrior chief in the seventh century, and carried him through many battles. The two were great companions, and were devoted to one another.

But then came the terrible occasion when the chief's young son – a boy of nine or ten years of age –mounted the horse and tried to ride it. This was a foolish experiment to try, as the huge horse needed much stronger adult hands to control it. The horse reared up in alarm and threw him off. The boy fell to the ground, and when his father rushed over to him, the boy was dead. The fall had broken his neck.

Holding the faithful horse guilty of killing his son, the chief was driven half insane with grief. He fetched his axe and slew the animal.

The White Horse of Leesthorpe Hill
(illustration by Julie Saunt)

The chief later came to regret his hasty reaction. He had not only lost his son in a terrible accident, but he had slaughtered his faithful steed the same day. The madness that had seized him that day had caused him to kill his wonderful horse, which was not in any way at fault. When the ghostly figure of the horse began to manifest itself, the chief took it as a sign of reproach for his hasty and intemperate action on the day of his son's death.

The horse has been seen gliding around the Leesthorpe area by many people, many of them motorists driving along the A606. In 1971, Marion and Greg Richardson were driving home from Oakham to Melton. When they came to Leesthorpe Hill, about two miles from Burton Lazars, a huge white shape hurtled across the road in front of them.

Startled, they stopped the car and began to speculate what they had witnessed. They agreed that it was shaped like a giant horse, but when Marion suggested that they'd seen a ghost, Greg was reluctant to accept this. He wanted a more rational explanation.

Over the next few weeks, Marion told everyone about her experience. A month after the event, an excited friend went into Marion's shop. A farmer from Leesthorpe had heard the friend relating the story about Marion and Greg, and he had told her the story of the White Horse which has haunted the area since the seventh century. Marion was just the latest of a long line of people who had seen it over the years.

THE HAUNTED POLICE STATION: *Syston*

In the summer of 1966, PC David Watson was on duty at Syston police station. Back then, there were always two policemen on

The Old Police Station at Syston
(illustration by Julie Saunt)

duty at night, one out on patrol walking round the village, making sure that all was well. The other – David on this occasion – was manning the station.

At 3.30am, he heard footsteps upstairs, and he assumed his colleague had come back to the police station, perhaps to use the loo, or to collect some more cigarettes.

The police station was based in an old manor house, with a grand, sweeping staircase. He walked over to the foot of the stairs and put all the lights on. To his astonishment, the footsteps came down the stairs and past him, but he could see no one attached to them. As the sound of the footsteps passed him, he felt an icy sensation, as if he were in a walk-in fridge.

The footsteps went into part of the police station that was used as the charge office and telephone switchboard. When the building was a manor house, this room had been a games room, with a large billiard table. The only souvenirs of those days were six chains hanging from the ceiling, which had originally held the lights suspended over the billiard table.

David followed the footsteps into the room and switched on the lights. There was nobody there. He then noticed that one of the hanging chains was swinging from side to side. This was a puzzle since it wasn't a windy night, and all the other doors and windows were shut. He found the whole episode peculiar, but decided not to tell any of his colleagues because they would 'take the mickey'.

However, some months later there was a course being held at Syston police station for cadets and new recruits. After the course, David saw an old, experienced bobby talking to a group of the young men. They seemed to be listening very intently, and hanging on the older man's every word. David sidled up so that he could hear what was being said.

'Years ago, when this was a manor house,' the old policeman was saying, 'there was a tragic event that took place here. The son of the lord of the manor committed suicide. And I'll tell you how he did it, lads,' he went on. 'He hanged himself from the light chains over the billiard table!'

David now believes that on that night in 1966 he must have experienced the ghost of the poor young man, the son of the lord of the manor, who had killed himself many years before.

BLACK ANNIS: *Dane Hills*

In Leicester, if children hadn't gone to sleep as soon as they were in bed, their mothers would shout, 'If you kids ain't asleep in five minutes, Black Annis'll come and eat yer!' The Black Annis referred to was a witch who lived in Dane Hills, an area between Leicester and Glenfield.

Annis had one eye, a blue face and long, sharp, pointed teeth. Her hands were actually sharp talons, which she used to kill her victims. She lived in a cave, eight feet wide and five feet high, which she had dug out with those powerful talons. In front of the cave was an oak tree, and Annis would hide in its branches, dropping down onto passers-by, before killing and eating them. The skins of her victims hung on the walls of the cave, and Annis used them to make her clothing. At least she was into recycling!

John Heyrick, a Leicestershire soldier and poet, who lived in the late 1700s, wrote:

Where down the plain the winding pathway falls
From Glenfield village to Leicester's ancient walls;
Nature or art with imitative power
Far in the glen has placed Black Annis's Bower.

The Original Bow Bridge
(illustration by Julie Saunt)

'Tis said the soul of mortal man recoiled
To view Black Annis's eye so fierce and wild.
Vast talons, foul with human flesh, there grew
In place of hands, and features vivid blue
Glared in her visage; whilst her obscene waist
Warm skins of human victims embraced.

When Annis failed to find humans for her dinner, she would hunt and eat hares. She could outrun the hares, and she ate them raw as soon as she caught them. Up until the eighteenth century, the Mayor of Leicester would attend an annual fair on Dane Hills, together with many other local worthies, on Easter

35

Monday. At midday, he would take part in the hunting of a hare. It seems highly likely that this killing of a hare was some kind of echo of the Black Annis story.

Annis also crops up in another local legend, when in 1485, King Richard III was riding out from Leicester at the head of his army to engage in battle with Henry Tudor at Bosworth Field. As he crossed Bow Bridge, Richard's heel struck the parapet, and Annis appeared in the crowd, shrieking out a message that 'Your heel has hit it on the way out, and your head will hit it on the way back in.' What the king made of this is not known, but when the two armies met at the Battle of Bosworth Field, Richard was killed. His corpse was thrown ignominiously over a horse and brought back to Leicester. Just as Black Annis had foretold, his body was brought across Bow Bridge and this time his head struck the parapet.

(Richard III's body was secretly buried at Greyfriars monastery, and has only recently been discovered under what is now a Leicester car park. His body will now be interred in Leicester Cathedral, only a few hundred yards away.)

In Victorian times, when melodramas were very popular, there were several plays written about Black Annis. One was entitled Black Anna's Bower or the Maniac of the Dane Hills, and Annis is of course the villainous maniac of the title. Interestingly, the name Cat Anna is still sometimes used in Leicester to describe a gossipy or unpleasant neighbour.

For many centuries no one wanted to live in Dane Hills, because of the scary reputation of Black Annis, so it was the late 1940s before houses were actually built there. On the very spot where

The Haunted Rupert's Gate at Leicester Castle
(photo by David Bell)

the notorious cave had been, houses now stand. Surely that ought to keep the witch down! Mind you, there is a story that a tunnel existed from the back of the cave that led all the way to Leicester Castle. That is some tunnelling, especially if it was dug using only talons, but there are accounts of Black Annis now appearing at the castle's Rupert's Gate. It is said that even the streetwise scared-of-nobody Leicester kids of today will not go there after dark, as – once again – the whisper is out: 'Black Annis will catch you and eat you!'

So the story is that Black Annis is an evil witch and a frightening cannibal. However, the poet and novelist Robert Graves describes the original Annis as a beautiful pagan goddess, worshipped in pre-Christian times. She was also called Anna, Anu or Danu. Graves also claims that Dane Hills – far from being a reference to the Vikings – was in fact called Danu's Hills, and the area was a sacred one. Annis was regarded as entirely benevolent. The pagan people loved and respected her, and she gave them plentiful harvests in return.

When Christianity first came to England, the early priests denounced Annis as an evil creature, and down the centuries it is this version of the Annis legend that survives. The children who half-believe this are part of a long tradition of Leicester people who accepted the version of Annis spread by the early church, when they were attempting to replace the pagan religion with Christianity.

Others try to reclaim her earlier reputation as a powerful but benevolent goddess, and there is a women's dancing troupe that proudly bears the name of Black Annis Women's Morris, who say, 'Black Annis was formed some time around 1982. We are an all-women team or "side", named after Leicester's famous witch who used to live in a cave in the Dane Hills area. We wear purple, green and white (suffragette colours), and have a bit of a reputation for being somewhat feisty. We have mellowed somewhat and although still feminists (what sensible woman isn't) we are slightly less loud and hard drinking than we used to be. One of our dance traditions is Humberstone Gate, a style unique to Black Annis and named after the Leicester street in which it was first danced.'

The dancers may be trying to resurrect the image of Black Annis as a benevolent goddess, but I'm afraid she is destined to be remembered in most of Leicester is as 'the witch who eats people'.

THE CAT AND THE CLEAVER: *Edmondthorpe*

The villagers of Edmondthorpe were all afraid of Lady Ann, the second wife of the elderly Sir Roger Smith. In the 1650s, the raven-haired Lady Ann must have been very exotic. She was very handsome, much younger than her husband – and she was Spanish. People said that if you looked into her dark eyes, she was able to read your thoughts.

When Sir Roger and Lady Ann returned from a visit to London, she sent for the butler and reprimanded him for allowing the servants to indulge in dancing and licentious revelry, both forbidden practices under the rule of Oliver Cromwell. She seemed to know in every minute detail exactly what had occurred during her absence, yet he knew that she hadn't spoken to anyone on her return.

Word quickly spread downstairs to the servants. It was true that they had made the most of the opportunity to enjoy themselves while the master and mistress were away, but how on earth did she know? They regarded Lady Ann with even more awe and terror than before.

A few weeks later, the butler was in the kitchen talking with the cook, who was cutting up joints of meat with a cleaver. The butler was telling the cook that he'd seen Lady Ann out riding at night, all alone. The two men began to snigger and speculate what she might have been up to. Was she meeting a man, a young lover? After all, her husband was very ancient.

As the two men gossiped and guffawed, the black cat that had been curled up on the window ledge sprang to its feet. It arched its back, then leapt at the butler, clawing at his face with savage intent. As the man reeled back, clutching his bleeding face, the cook came to his aid. He lashed out at the cat with the cleaver he was holding, causing a deep gash on its left front paw.

The cat fled, leaving a trail of blood on the flagstones. The two men followed the trail until it petered out, but they could find no sign of the cat. It seemed to have disappeared into thin air. Later the cook tried to scrub the kitchen floor, but somehow the bloodstains proved resistant to his efforts.

That evening, the butler was serving dinner, and he noticed that Lady Ann appeared ill, her face pale and wan. To his horror, he noticed that her left wrist was injured and bandaged. He opened his mouth to tell Sir Roger about the earlier event in the kitchen, and to draw a parallel between the injury to the cat's left front

The Monument of Lady Ann Smith in Edmonthorpe Church
(photo by David Bell)

paw and Lady Ann's injured left wrist. However, as Lady Ann's hypnotic dark eyes gazed into his, he found himself unable to speak. Lady Ann, he concluded, was the cat. She could transform into a cat when it suited her. He had better hold his tongue.

The bloodstained flagstone was never able to be scrubbed clean. In 1919, two hundred and fifty years later, it was taken up, and carried to the neighbouring village of Wymondham, where it was displayed in the workshop of J W Golling.

An even more interesting reminder of the story can be seen in Edmondthorpe church. There is an alabaster monument of Sir Roger Smith and his two wives. On the figure of Lady Ann, his second wife, visitors can still see a red stain spreading over the folds of her costume, seemingly issuing from her left wrist.

THE BLEEDING TOMB: Hinckley

**A FATAL HALBERD HIS MORTAL BODY SLEW
THE MURDERING HAND GOD'S VENGEANCE
WILL PURSUE
FROM SHADES TERRESTIAL.
THOUGH JUSTICE TOOK HER FLIGHT
SHALL NOT THE JUDGE OF ALL THE WORLD
DO RIGHT?
EACH AGE AND SEX HIS INNOCENCE BEMOANS
AND WITH SAD SIGHS LAMENT HIS DYING
GROANS.**

This epitaph on a gravestone in St Mary's churchyard in Hinckley is a reminder of a terrible event in the town's history.

It was 17th April 1727, and a crowd of Hinckley townsmen were standing outside an inn, The George and Dragon. They were being harangued by a visiting recruiting sergeant. He was a tough old campaigner in his scarlet and gold uniform. He tried persuading them with tales of the fine life to be had if they enlisted as soldiers, but to no avail. The Hinckley people remained unimpressed.

Annoyed, he tried another tack. Growing red in the face, and waving his halberd, he started to spin dark threats of what would happen to Hinckley if the Old Pretender, James Stuart, were to sweep down from Scotland with his papist hordes, to reclaim the English throne for the Stuarts. All of the men would be butchered and their wives and children would be burned alive in their houses.

Still no one seemed to take him seriously. One of the listeners, a twenty-year-old saddler named Richard Smith, began to question what the sergeant was saying. Not all Catholics were bad, he pointed out, and in any case people hadn't been butchered and burned when James Stuart's father was on the throne.

The recruiting sergeant was not used to having his words challenged. When he spoke, men usually jumped to obey. He began to lose his temper, to swear and curse at the crowd. He had taken a few pints of ale earlier in the day. Turning to Richard, he bellowed out that if the young man had any patriotism or courage, he would join the army and fight for England, for the Protestant religion and for King George.

The Bleeding Tomb of Richard Smith
(photo by David Bell)

He glanced up at the inn sign and laughed triumphantly. 'You'll all drink beer in the George', he yelled, 'but you won't fight for King George!' That should put his heckler in his place, he concluded.

Not in the least abashed, the young saddler had an answer. Quite reasonable, he pointed out that the inn sign was a picture of Saint George, not King George. The crowd began to cheer and clap. They were laughing at the old soldier.

In a state of blind fury, the sergeant levelled his halberd and charged at Richard Smith. The weapon entered the young man's chest, went through him and impaled him to a tree. The shocked townspeople stared in horror at the dying Richard, cruelly pinned to the tree. The sergeant sobered up very quickly and decided to quit Hinckley. He left the town very quickly, and was never seen again.

Every year, in April, drops of red liquid can be seen running down the gravestone of Richard Smith, and people say that the tombstone is bleeding because his killer was never caught.

THE HAUNTED THEATRE: *Market Harborough*

The theatre in Church Square, Market Harborough, has long had a reputation for being haunted. Many of the volunteers who work there have reported strange experiences. Ann Sagger has heard footsteps, Trevor Brown has heard singing, and Norman

The Haunted Theatre at Market Harborough
(photo by David Bell)

Ward has heard groans and creaks, on all three occasions while that person was alone in the theatre.

On one occasion, the theatre group bought a brand new top-quality recording tape, but when they began to use it, they heard the voice of a mysterious woman singing a sad lament. No one knew who she was, but they all thought the song sounded as if it were from a previous age.

One July, Ann Window and her mother-in-law Viv had volunteered to clear out the costume space, situated underneath the seats of the auditorium. Ann was actually in the wardrobe space, while Viv was vacuuming the area between the seating and the theatre foyer.

When Viv heard footsteps walking on the wooden floor along the back row of the seats, she naturally assumed that another volunteer had come in. Then she realised that nobody had passed her and, in any case, the theatre doors were locked. She then wondered if the footsteps were some kind of echo of Ann working in the costume store below the seats.

Viv went to find Ann, but she was standing on a concrete floor and hadn't been walking about. Ann said that she had heard the footsteps too, just above her head, and had assumed they were Viv's. They both had to conclude that, since it was neither of them, it must be the well-known theatre ghost. Viv told me that she has never felt frightened of the ghost, and always calls out a greeting to it when she enters the empty building.

The Harborough Theatre was opened in 1933, and was converted from a cycle shed attached to a factory. However, the building was originally an inn called the Green Dragon. Back in 1791, a maid named Hannah Buswell lived and worked at the inn. She was 17 years old, and although she had a lover, John Bell, she liked to flirt with the customers who frequented the Green Dragon. This used to make John, a young apprentice, very jealous, and they often used to quarrel about her flirtatiousness.

After one particularly loud and violent row, Hannah disappeared and was never seen again. The suspicion that her lover had harmed her, perhaps even killed her, was strengthened when he left town the next day. Although his master, a baker, sent word all round the locality that he would welcome John's return to work, the boy never did come back to Market Harborough.

It was thought that if John had killed Hannah, he might have disposed of her body in the River Welland, before running away. Indeed a woman's body was found some weeks later in the river some ten miles downstream, at the weir at Middleton Mill. The body was assumed to be that of a vagrant and was buried before anyone could check if it actually was that of Hannah Buswell.

The theatre group often conjecture whether their ghost could be that of Hannah, still haunting the building where she lived and worked. Could it be Hannah's footsteps that Viv and Ann heard, and Hannah's voice singing the sad old song somehow recorded on tape?

BUTTERFLY HALL: *Lubenham*

In its day, Papillon Hall had the reputation of being the most haunted house in Leicestershire. It was situated on the old A427 (now the A4304), the road from Market Harborough to Lutterworth, about a mile west of Lubenham. It was erected in 1624, substantially altered in 1903, and demolished in 1950. Many of the hall's hauntings date back to David Papillon, the great-grandson of the original builder. Although a handsome man, he had an awe-inspiring personality. The local people were terrified of him and called him 'Lord Pamp', an old name for the devil. Papillon Hall has been known as Pamps ever since that time.

Papillon Hall

Pamp had the power of fixing people: putting them into a hypnotic trance. Once he came across some men who were making a poor job of ploughing one of his fields, so he fixed them. They were unable to move at all until he came back at dusk and released them. Another example was when a footpad attempted to rob him as he rode home from Market Harborough with a bag of money for wages Pamp fixed the would-be thief, leaving him unable to move, then rode home.

A portrait of David Papillon, aged 24, was painted in 1715. This painting has had a peculiar effect on people ever since, including many who knew nothing of the stories surrounding Lord Pamp. In 1800, a maidservant girl was woken in the night by a sound. To her horror, she saw Lord Pamp standing by the foot of her bed. He was dressed exactly as in his portrait, in a red coat and gold waistcoat, convincing her that he had emerged from the picture.

By 1840, Papillon Hall was lived in by a Mr Marriot. He begged Thomas Papillon to remove the portrait of his ancestor because of its sinister influence. He said that no servants would work at the Hall, because Pamp used to come out of the painting and molest them. Thomas Papillon agreed and the picture was removed. But even after Papillon Hall was demolished in 1950, Mr and Mrs Hewes, the owners of Papillon Farm, claimed that their stables were still haunted by Pamp.

The original Papillon Hall was an octagonal building standing on raised ground. It had four attics, one of them known as Pamp's attic. This attic was bricked up with just a small entrance hatch. Before he married in 1717, Pamp had kept a mistress, a lady of Spanish descent. She died in 1715, two years before his

David Papillon of Papillon Hall, known as "Pamp" locally.
The haunting picture painted in 1716

marriage, but there is no local record of her burial. When Captain Frank Belville bought the house in 1903, he decided to have it altered and extended. Edwin Lutyens was engaged, and decided to add four wings to the square building to make it resemble a butterfly. Papillon is, of course, the French word for butterfly, so Papillon Hall is really Butterfly Hall. It was during these alterations that the skeleton of a woman – almost certainly that of the Spanish mistress – was found in the bricked-up attic. It is to be hoped that she was dead before being bricked up in the attic.

The Spanish lady had prophesied that ill fortune would occur if her dancing shoes ever left the Hall. The belief in this curse was so strong that whenever the house changed hands, the deeds required the new owners to keep the shoes in Papillon Hall. These shoes – actually a pair of silver and green brocade slippers fitted into a pair of patterns – were the source of more supernatural events at the hall. When Thomas Halford was residing at the Hall, he allowed the shoes to be taken to an exhibition in Paris. Life at Papillon Hall became so intolerable, with nocturnal crashing noises and groans, that the family moved out of the house until the shoes were able to come back.

When another owner, George Bosworth, died in 1866, the shoes were bequeathed to his daughter in Leicester. At Papillon Hall, the disturbances recommenced and terrified the family of the new owner. They continued every night until the shoes were returned to Pamps. Only then was peace restored. A later owner had a strong cupboard constructed for them in the wall above the main fireplace, with a padlocked grille for a door.

When Captain Belville was having the Lutyens alterations made, he had the shoes removed for safe keeping during the building work. Immediately all hell broke loose at Papillon Hall. Several builders were injured and eventually one was killed. No local men would work at Pamps, and Lutyens had to import workmen from further away. Belville himself sustained a back injury when his pony-trap mysteriously turned over, and he decided enough was enough. He retrieved the shoes from his solicitors' office and restored them to their place in the house. Peace was temporarily restored.

However, five years later he was foolish enough to lend the shoes to Leicester Museum. In the days that followed, three polo ponies were killed by lightning, the Hall caught fire, two servants died, and Captain Belville fractured his skull while hunting. The shoes were immediately fetched home, locked behind the grille, and the key was thrown into the lake.

During World War II the Hall was occupied by American servicemen from the 82nd Airborne division. Some of the men, knowing that every day might be their last, decided to test the superstition. The grille was smashed open and, on at least two occasions, a shoe was taken away. Each time, the man who took the shoe was killed, and his friends brought the shoe back to Pamps.

When the Hall was demolished in 1950, the two shoes were sent to descendants of the Papillon family in Sussex. With the curse on the dancing shoes, and the hypnotic Lord Pamp who came out of his portrait at night to molest the maidservants, it is easy to see why Papillon Hall – Butterfly Hall – was regarded as the most haunted place in the county.

BRAUNSTONE HALL: *Leicester*

Although Papillon Hall at Lubenham has always claimed to be the county's most haunted house, Braunstone Hall must be an equal contender. The hall was built in 1776 for the Winstanley family, and they lived there until 1926. Rosemary Winstanley was born there in 1914, the third of six children. She lived in the nursery wing on the top storey, which was run by the nanny, Mrs Hattersley, and the nursery maid, Bessie.

Rosemary was eight when she first saw the ghost of a lady in white walking along the long passageway that led to the nursery, but it was a few years later that the children were awakened by the nursery maid screaming in the night. Bessie insisted that she'd seen a young woman in a white veil and a long white robe, bending over her.

Rosemary was an adult before she learned that her father's two sisters, May and Georgina, had entered a convent when they were 17 and 19 respectively. Tragically, the younger of them died of TB a year later while she was still a novice. It might be relevant to note that, as a novice, she would have worn a white robe. Moreover, the room where the ghost in a veil had appeared to the maid was May's old room. Rosemary is convinced that the ghost is that of her young aunt, May, who has returned to her childhood home.

Braunstone Hall became a school in 1932, and it was the home of Braunstone Hall Junior School until 1996, serving children

Braunstone Hall
(photo by David Bell)

from the local area. Alan Jarvis was the school caretaker from 1973 until 1985, and he saw the lady in white one evening at 5pm, while he was cleaning the top floor. He called out to her, but when she floated towards him, he dropped his brushes and fled.

Alan's daughter, Shirley, became the school secretary. In April 1989 she spent a night in the building with her sister, Llyn, and some members of the Leicester University Psychic Studies Fellowship. They experienced a number of ghosts that night. One member, Garth, saw both the lady in white and another lady in a pink ballgown. They also saw a little girl hiding in the attic and a man dressed like a gamekeeper, in rough leather knee-length trousers. At 3.30am another member of the group, James, saw the white lady move along the corridor and enter a classroom. He fetched two others and all three of them saw her standing to the right of the blackboard. This classroom has been the centre of the building's haunting, and passers-by have reported a light coming from the room during the night.

None of the ghosts hold any terrors for Rosemary Richardson, née Rosemary Winstanley, who intends to become one of their number. In 1976 she wrote, 'Braunstone Hall was one of the great loves of my life, and I never got over having to leave my birthplace when I was twelve. I dare say that after my death I shall return to Braunstone.'

THE HAUNTED RAILWAY LINE: *Wykin*

The haunting of the footpath that was formerly a railway line in south-west Leicestershire began just over a hundred and fifty years ago. An elderly lady from Higham-on-the-Hill was walking towards Wykin with her pet terrier dog, Scottie. When she came to a suitable spot where there were no houses and no people about, she let the dog off his lead for a run. She had done this quite frequently without any problems with the animal, but on this occasion the mischievous Scottie ran off into the fields and refused to come back. She searched the fields, still calling out for Scottie to come back, but there was no sign of the disobedient terrier.

She decided that it must have gone down onto the small railway line that was only used for carrying coal. In a state of distress, she walked along the road until she came to a gap in the high hedge. She pushed her way through the hedge and began to walk along the railway track, whistling and calling the dog's name. As she was rather deaf and was concentrating on the task of finding her dog, she didn't hear the coal train coming up behind her. The engine driver applied his brakes as soon as he saw her, but he was too late. The engine hit the old lady, killing her instantly.

A few months after the terrible accident, people began to talk of hearing a female voice calling out on the railway line between Wykin and Higham-on-the-Hill. No one ever managed to see who was doing the calling. Because the voice was clearly that of an elderly lady, and because it seemed to be calling for her dog

The haunted railway track at Wykin
(illustration by Julie Saunt)

to come back, the belief soon grew that it was the ghost of the old lady, still walking the track searching for her dog.

The haunting has gone on ever since. Although the railway track was taken up some decades ago, the lady's voice is still heard along the footpath that replaced it. The dog itself never turned up, and some people claim that when they have heard the lady's ghostly voice calling out for the terrier, they have also heard the faint sound of barking in the distance.

CAUGHT ON CAMERA: *Belgrave Hall*

For a number of years, people have been seeing ghosts at Belgrave Hall, a three-storey building situated just two miles north of Leicester city centre. The ghosts are dressed in Victorian costume, and one of the ghosts is said to be that of Charlotte, the daughter of John Ellis, a former owner of the house.

The Hall was built between 1709 and 1713 for Edmund Cradock, who unfortunately died soon after its completion, and it passed out of the family in 1715. John Ellis moved into the Hall in 1846 with his wife and eight children. He was a wealthy businessman who was responsible for bringing the railways to Leicester. He was a Quaker, and his family took an active part in local charities and in politics. His daughters, including Charlotte, were said to be among the most educated women in Leicester.

The ghost of Charlotte Ellis is not the only one to haunt Belgrave Hall. Staff members have reported seeing the ghosts of three different Victorian ladies in the Hall itself and also in the two-acre walled garden. They have also smelled the aroma of fresh-baked bread, when no cooking is taking place.

In 1936 it was purchased by Leicester Corporation for use as a museum and botanical gardens, showing the contrasting lifestyles of a Victorian upper-middle-class family and its domestic servants. In 1999, two ghostly figures were recorded at 4.50am on security cameras immediately outside the hall. This was reported in the press, and caused a great deal of attention.

Belgrave Hall
(photo by David Bell)

Belgrave Hall became famous across the world, and featured on several television programmes, including Most Haunted and Paranormal Files.

Stuart Warburton, the curator of the museum, stated, 'The security cameras at the back of the hall triggered off one night at about 4.50am, and then suddenly two figures appear on the film. The camera freezes for about five seconds and then the figures disappear. The hall is haunted, there is no question about that.'

Stuart decided to have the International Society of Paranormal Research come to Belgrave Hall to investigate the phenomenon. The ISPR decided that the outside images captured on the security cameras were caused by natural environmental factors, but they confirmed that the hall itself was a site of considerable paranormal activity.

Apart from the three female ghosts, they found a ghost of a man who had died in a fall, and another of a child that had died of TB. Although the ISPR members had no knowledge of the former residents of Belgrave Hall, both of these ghosts corresponded with people who had died there. They also felt the presence of a 'male negative energy' upstairs that was so powerful that they decided not to disturb it any further.

THE BATTLE OF BOSWORTH REVISITED

Joanna Dessau, a retired head teacher, was on her way to Cadeby, Leicestershire. It was a sunny August day in the early 1980s, and she was on a coach of people on their way to a traction engine rally. The local vicar of Cadeby church was the late Teddy Boston, a great enthusiast for steam engines.

As the coach arrived at the traction rally, Mrs Dessau experienced a very strange phenomenon. For the rest of the coach passengers the day remained fine and sunny, but for Joanna the sun went in, the sky became gloomy and a cold wind sprang up. She could see nothing of the rally, but saw only great trees looming over her.

To the alarm of her friends, she began to call out that she needed a horse and she had to get to 'the hill'. She had to be forcibly restrained from clambering through a hedge. It was assumed that she had been taken ill, perhaps with sunstroke.

She was out of it for over two hours. She later reported that she was surrounded by grey sky, and was hearing terrible sounds: men's voices shouting, the clash of swords on armour, men screaming and groaning. These were the sounds of an old battle.

Then, out of nowhere, she was back with her friends at the rally, in the bright sunshine. Her companions were very relieved to have her back to normality, her distressing behaviour completely disappeared.

Joanna writes, 'I should point out that I had not known my destination and did not discover it until this experience was over.

The Statue of Richard III in Castle Park (photo by David Bell)

Well, of course, the hill was the hill of the Battle of Bosworth, and it was only 1½ miles from the field where the rally was being held. What is more, the battle was fought on that very date in unseasonably dark and chilly August weather. And the battle had lasted 2½ hours! What is more, while in floods of tears quite inexplicable to my companions, I had correctly pointed out the exact route taken by King Richard's body after the battle.'

Joanna had no idea that the date of the trip to the traction rally – 22nd August – was the anniversary of the Battle of Bosworth in 1485. She has been back since, but to her relief she did not repeat her earlier frightening experience.

King Richard's body was taken to Leicester, where it was secretly buried. In 2012 a body was found under a car park in Leicester, and by comparing its DNA with those of a descendant of the king's sister, it has been proved that the remains are those of Richard III. I wonder whether his disinterment might trigger more phenomena like that experienced by Joanna Dessau.

ESMERALDA, THE GYPSY GIRL: *Stoke Golding*

The Three Horseshoes inn in Stoke Golding is haunted by the ghost of a gypsy girl called Esmeralda. Her story goes back to 1910, when a group of gypsies were camping near the village. Women from the camp were going from door to door, trying to sell lucky heather, pegs and lace.

When young Emeralda came to the Three Horseshoes, she went round the back to find the door. Unfortunately the large flat stone that covered the well at the back of the inn had been taken off and not replaced. The poor girl didn't notice, tripped and fell into the well. The innkeeper's family heard her screams and rushed out to help, but they were too late. The girl had drowned.

He family and friends collected her body and took it away for a gypsy funeral, and put a curse on the well. It was not a curse on the innkeeper and his family – they had tried to save Esmeralda – nor on the inn and its patrons. The curse was very specifically on the well.

Nothing resulted from this for over sixty years. No one saw anything that suggested the place was haunted. However, in the 1970s alterations to the inn were made. The well was slabbed over and an extension to the inn was built. The well was now directly under the newer part of the inn, including the restaurant and kitchen.

And from this time, strange happenings occurred.

The Three Horseshoes Inn at Stoke Golding
(photo by David Bell)

In the kitchen the lights would suddenly dim for no apparent reason, and the staff would notice a drop in the temperature. They also had a sensation that they were being watched, although they couldn't see or hear anyone there.

But there was one occasion when guests in the Three Horseshoes did see the figure of a young woman in gypsy costume gliding effortlessly across the lounge, almost as if she were floating. As they gazed, open-mouthed, she disappeared through the wall.

Both the customers on this occasion and the kitchen staff have commented that the phenomena they experience – the dimming of the lights, the sudden cold, the feeling of being observed and the one-time appearance of the young gypsy girl crossing the lounge – are not scary. They have a feeling of goodwill being directed towards them. It seems that Esmeralda likes them, and is well disposed towards them. Perhaps she approves of the inn getting rid of the well where she died.

TOPSY TURVEY: *Bilstone*

Topsy Turvey was a Leicestershire wrestler who boasted that he could turn any opponent upside down – topsy-turvy – and throw them over his head. He lived in the hamlet of Bilstone, only a few miles from the spot where Leicestershire, Derbyshire, Staffordshire and Warwickshire all meet.

His real name was John Massey, and he was a hedger and ditcher. He enjoyed a reputation as a hard, brutal man and a prolific drinker. He was a widower, and in 1799 he married his second wife, a widow with a ten-year-old daughter.

One afternoon, Topsy Turvey was walking home after a session in the local pub, when he met his new wife. Nobody knows what she said to him; perhaps 'I've given your dinner to the dog' or 'Look at the state of you!' Whatever it was, it angered the man and he began to beat his wife so hard that

The Mill Race at Bilstone Watermill
(photo by David Bell)

she fell to the ground with a broken leg. He then did no more than pick her up, carried her to the village watermill and threw her into the mill race, where she drowned. His stepdaughter tried to intervene, so he threw her in too, but she swam to the bank and survived to give evidence against Massey when he was tried in Leicester for murder.

The judge at his trial – Baron Vaughan – sentenced him to death, at which moment Topsy Turvey came out with a crass request. Would they bury him between his two wives? When you consider that he'd killed one of them, this was somewhat impudent. He did not get his way, because after he'd been hanged at Red Hill near Birstall, his dead body was taken back to Bilstone, fastened in iron chains, and suspended from a gibbet.

The gibbet is still there and can be seen on the road from Twycross to Bilstone, the road being called, not surprisingly, Gibbet Lane. It is a seven-foot post surrounded by a small fence, and bearing a notice with details of the crime.

I used to think that a hanged man was left on a gibbet for a few weeks, to show what happened to evil men. However, John Massey's body remained on the gibbet at Bilstone for eighteen years! Eventually his skull was stolen and taken over the county border into Atherstone. I have heard from two sources that it is now kept in the safe of a pub in the back streets of that town, and only comes out on Shrove Tuesday, following the town's annual mass football event.

The Gibbet Post at Bilstone
(photo by David Bell)

There are a number of stories connected with the gibbet post. One lady tells me that the people who now live in Bilstone watermill have often heard a splash in the dead of night, as if a body is once more being thrown into the mill race.

However, the most fascinating story was told to me by a lady from Birmingham. She had heard of the gibbet post at Bilstone and wanted to see it. It did take her some years to track it down, because she thought it was in Bilston in the Black Country. When she did discover that it was at a hamlet near Twycross in Leicestershire, she decided to drive over to see it. She arrived there, and got out to note down the information on the notice board. 'There was a lady there looking at the gibbet post. I nodded to her but she didn't speak. She had a little girl with her, but she was skipping around and not taking any notice.'

When the Birmingham lady was halfway back to Birmingham, a sudden thought struck her. She told me, 'I suddenly wondered why the lady and girl were dripping wet when it hadn't rained all day!' She is now convinced that she'd seen the ghost of the murdered woman and her daughter. This supposition was made more certain when she developed the photos she had taken of the post, and found no sign of the lady or the girl.

FOOTSTEPS AND A SCREAMING BABY:

Breedon-on-the-Hill

In Breedon-on-the-Hill, the church that stands on top of the hill has an unusual name: it is dedicated to St Mary and St Hardulph. It stands overlooking a large working quarry, and can be seen from many miles around.

Until the mid-1960s a residence known as Platchetts House stood there too. Platchetts House had been built in 1790, and it was the home of Harold and Norah Kirby from 1952 until 1966, when it was demolished by the quarry company.

Breedon Church Situated on top of the quarry
© Richard Green

One evening, Norah and Harold and their other children had gone to bed, leaving their nineteen-year-old daughter Pat studying downstairs. They had left the landing light on, for Pat to switch off when she came up. Some time later, Norah and Harold heard footsteps come up the stairs, and they naturally assumed it was Pat coming up to bed. When she realised that the landing light was still on, Norah naturally assumed that Pat had forgotten to switch it off. She got out of bed and looked into Pat's room, but her daughter was not there. Norah went downstairs and found Pat had fallen asleep over her books in the chair. So the footsteps on the stairs hadn't been hers. Norah wasn't the only one who'd heard the unexplained sounds, because the next day her other daughter, Jo, confirmed that she too had heard the footsteps coming up the stairs.

When Norah's mother was staying at Platchetts, she said that she had also heard footsteps on the stairs on several occasions. These footsteps were going down the stairs, then along the stone path under the front window. Every time, she recalled, there were eleven footsteps on the stairs, then thirteen outside. This pattern of footsteps was also heard by Norah's aunt when she was at Platchetts House.

The other strange manifestation that Norah heard was on the path that led from Platchetts House to the church. She was out at dusk, walking the dogs, when she heard a baby. 'It was not just crying,' Norah told me. 'It was really terrified screaming.' Alarmed, she tried to find the baby, following the sounds to the spot where they were coming from, but there was nothing to be seen.

Norah doesn't know whether the two phenomena – footsteps and the screaming baby – are in any way connected. However, when the house was demolished in 1966, human bones were discovered under the garden.

GHOST ON A BIKE: *Measham*

Dave Lindsey, a service engineer, was on his way to mend someone's washing machine in Twycross. It was noon on a drizzly day in 1975. He was driving down Gallows Lane in Measham, and he halted when he came to the staggered junction with Leicester Road. He glanced left and saw 'a typical Measham bloke on a bike'. The man had on a flat cap, his snap bag on his handlebars, and was cycling along at about half-a-mile per hour.

Dave sat waiting, no doubt tapping his fingers on his steering wheel, until the man had passed in front of his van. He looked left – there was nothing else coming – then glanced right. To Dave's surprise, there was no sign of the cyclist. He had only glanced away for a second and, at the speed the bike was travelling, it should have been only a few yards away. Thinking the man might have fallen off his bike, Dave got out of his van and began to look for the vanished cyclist. He checked the sunken footpath opposite, and he even made sure that the bike hadn't suddenly turned right, back up Gallows Lane. There were no houses nearby where the man might have gone.

Puzzled, he got back into his van and carried on to Twycross. But in the weeks that followed, whenever he was in the Measham/Twycross area, he always mentioned the man on a bike who had simply disappeared. The reply was always the same. In a phlegmatic tone of voice, he would be told, 'Oh, don't worry about that, me duck. You've just seen the ghost of the cycling miner. No end of folk have seen him.'

I thought that was the end of the matter, until I wrote about the story in a local paper. I was immediately contacted by a Leonard Hogg from Woodville, who told me that he thought the ghost was that of his father, George. 'My dad was a miner at Measham pit,' he explained, 'and he was killed on his bike in the war, during the blackout. I think the man that hit him had been drinking, but they didn't have breathalysers back then.' When I said that I hoped my writing about the ghost on a bike hadn't caused him any distress, he put me at my ease by saying, 'No. My dad was a big believer in ghosts. If there is such a thing, he'd definitely want to be one.' Then he added, 'Anyway, I like to think of him still biking round Measham.'

THE GHOST OF A NINE-DAYS-QUEEN:

Newtown Linford

If you should visit Bradgate Park on a dark winter evening, you will need more than your fair share of courage. As you walk between the stone outcrops, the pollarded trees and the ruins of Bradgate Hall, you will repeatedly glance over your shoulder, for Bradgate Park was the home of Lady Jane Grey, the nine-days-queen of England.

Jane was, through her mother, the great-niece of King Henry VIII. She was born at Groby Manor, but her family moved to Bradgate Hall while she was still a baby. She was a bright girl, and was very well educated. At the age of 15, she was fluent in seven languages. But the fact that she was fifth in line to the throne led to her terrible death. Henry VIII had died and his young son Edward was on the throne. Edward was a sickly boy and died at the age of sixteen. The next in line to the throne was his elder sister Mary, but many were afraid that she would take England back to the Roman Catholic religion and punish those who had supported the Protestant cause.

The Earl of Northumberland saw a way of becoming a power behind the throne. He plotted with Lady Jane Grey's father that Jane should marry his son, Lord Dudley. The fifteen-year-old girl was not keen, but her father thrashed her until she agreed. On the death of the boy king, they proclaimed Jane queen of England. However she only reigned for nine days.

Mary had a greater claim to the throne, and many of the nobles who had proclaimed Jane as queen, turned up nine days later to proclaim Queen Mary. She immediately returned England to Catholicism and set about the execution of all those who had opposed her, including the Earl of Northumberland. She killed so many that she was soon called Bloody Mary.

She did not kill Lady Jane Grey immediately, but had her and her husband imprisoned in the Tower of London. A year later however, after several plots against her, Bloody Mary decided that a living Lady Jane was a focus for rebellion. She therefore had Jane and her husband put to death. Lord Dudley was hanged, but young Jane was taken to the block and publically beheaded. She was still only sixteen years old.

When Jane was beheaded, her family had the poplar trees on the avenue up to Bradgate Hall pollarded. Their tops were taken off as a mark of mourning and remembrance of the beheaded girl.

On New Year's Eve, a ghostly carriage pulled by four horses and carrying the solitary figure of a young woman, has been seen travelling through the village of Newtown Linford. When it gets to the church, it vanishes completely, only to reappear nine days later. The carriage then continues up to the ruins of Bradgate House, and the ghost of Lady Jane Grey alights. The nine-days-queen has returned to her childhood home.

BIBLIOGRAPHY

THE FOLKLORE OF LEICS AND RUTLAND
Roy Palmer 1985
HISTORY AND ANTIQUITIES OF THE COUNTY OF
LEICESTER John Nichols 1804
HOLY WELLS AND SPRINGS OF LEICESTERSHIRE
AND RUTLAND Bob Trubshaw 1990
STANDING STONES AND MARK STONES OF LEICS
& RUTLAND Bob Trubshaw 1991
LEICESTERSHIRE & RUTLAND GHOSTS & LEGENDS
David Bell 1992
THE HISTORY OF THE MYSTERIOUS PAPILLON
HALL Colonel Pen Lloyd 1977
ROYAL HAUNTINGS Joan Forman 1987

THANKS

I would like to give thanks for help given by Julie Saunt,
Richard Green, Colin Crosby, Bob Trubshaw, Jake Young,
Ruth Wallhead, Chris and Graham Bell, Joan Leatherland,
Neil Lewis, Emma Ellis and Len Holden.

Other **GHOST STORIES** for you to enjoy from
BRADWELL BOOKS

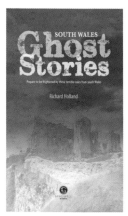